SHAWN GREEN
LOS ANGELES
DODGERS ◇4

HANK GREENBERG

ART SHAMSKY OUTFIELD

REDS

GABE KAPLER
TEXAS RANGERS

VANKEES

RON BLOMBERG

BROWNS

DELTY ST. LOUIS AMER

39

MIKE LIBERTHAL

TOP PROSPECT

STL

STONE ST. LOUIS

HARRY "THE HORSE" DANNING

HAMMERIN' HANK

THE LIFE OF HANK GREENBERG

YONA ZELDIS McDONOUGH
ILLUSTRATIONS BY MALCAH ZELDIS

WALKER & COMPANY ✳ NEW YORK

FOR JAMES REDDEN McDONOUGH, STAR PLAYER, STELLAR SON —Y. Z. M.

FOR MARNEE MAY AND TO THE MEMORY OF MY BROTHER,
JACK BRIGHTMAN —M. Z.

Text copyright © 2006 by Yona Zeldis McDonough
Illustrations copyright © 2006 by Malcah Zeldis

First published in the United States of America in 2006 by Walker Publishing Company, Inc.
Distributed to the trade by Holtzbrinck Publishers

For information about permission to reproduce selections from
this book, write to Permissions, Walker & Company,
104 Fifth Avenue, New York, New York 10011.

Library of Congress Cataloging-in-Publication Data
McDonough, Yona Zeldis.
Hammerin' Hank: the story of Hank Greenberg / Yona Zeldis McDonough; illustrations by Malcah Zeldis
p. cm.
Includes bibliographical references.
ISBN—10: 0-8027-8997-8 (hardcover)
ISBN—13: 978-0-8027-8997-6 (hardcover)
ISBN—10: 0-8027-8998-6 (reinforced)
ISBN—13: 978-0-8027-8998-3 (reinforced)
1. Greenberg, Hank—Juvenile literature. 2. Baseball players—United States—Biography—Juvenile literature.
3. Detroit Tigers (Baseball team)—History—Juvenile literature. I. Zeldis, Malcah, ill. II. Title.

GV865.G68M36 2006   796.357'092—dc22   [B]   2005048639

The artist used gouache on watercolor paper to create the illustrations for this book.

Book design by John Candell

WHEATIES is a registered trademark of General Mills, Inc.

Visit Walker & Company's Web site at www.walkeryoungreaders.com

Printed in China

10 9 8 7 6 5 4 3 2 1

Once there was a baseball player who was tall, strong, and handsome. He also happened to be Jewish. Many people who watched baseball then thought that Jews—like blacks, Asians, and Hispanics—weren't "real" Americans. For them, baseball was an American game. These people gave the Jewish ballplayer a hard time. They called him terrible names while he played and insulted him when he was off the field. But still, he kept on playing because baseball was the thing he loved most in the world. His name was Hank Greenberg and here is his story.

Henry Benjamin Greenberg was born on January 1, 1911, in New York City. His parents, David and Sarah, were Orthodox Jews. His father owned the Acme Textile Shrinking Works—a company that shrank cloth before it was made into suits—and his mother kept house. With four children, she was always busy. So busy that Hank and his siblings had plenty of freedom. For Hank, this meant freedom to play baseball.

When Hank was seven, his family moved from Greenwich Village, in Manhattan, to the Bronx. After school, he'd rush off to nearby Crotona Park with his ball, glove, and bat. He didn't come home until dark. On weekends, he'd fill his pockets with fruit and candy and stay down at the ballpark all day. Remembering those times, Hank said, "We were just in love with playing baseball, and the days weren't long enough."

Hank was tall. At thirteen, he was already six foot three inches, taller than many men. Kids teased him and he felt clumsy. Even adults made comments. And he had a bad case of acne—pimples—that made him feel even worse about himself.

Sports were an escape. In high school, he played soccer and basketball, too. But baseball remained his favorite game. When he played, his height was no longer a problem. He felt less clumsy with a ball in his hand. Yet Hank wasn't a natural athlete. Things didn't come easily to him. One of his coaches, Irwin Dickstein, said, "Hank never *played* games, he *worked* at them." It was true. His reactions were slow, and he had trouble coordinating his body. But because he loved the game, he kept practicing until he improved.

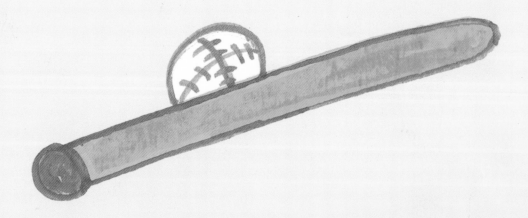

Hank's parents didn't approve of baseball. It wasn't a respectable profession—the men who played it were pretty rowdy. His parents thought he should go to college, to become a doctor, lawyer, or schoolteacher. His mother used to ask why he was wasting his time. "It's a bum's game," she said.

Hank enrolled in New York University, where he was given a basketball scholarship. He dropped out after a single semester. "Pop," he told his disappointed father, "I've got to play baseball." Despite his parents' disapproval and his own handicaps, Hank was going to try to make a life for himself in baseball.

He tried out for the New York Giants, a major league team, but the manager thought Hank was too big and uncoordinated. The New York Yankees finally recruited Hank for their minor league team. This meant if he worked hard, he might be called up to the Yankees' major league team. But Hank turned down the Yankees' offer; he thought there would be little chance of his making the major league with the powerful Lou Gehrig on the team. Instead, in January 1930, he signed with the Detroit Tigers. The boy from the Bronx was going to see—and play for—America.

Hank spent the next three years in the minor leagues, working hard every day to improve his fielding and hitting. It wasn't easy. In 1932, he was asked to be a third baseman. He had been playing first base and hadn't played third since he was a kid.

"I put on a fielder's glove and worked like a dog," Hank recalled. "I'd never used anything but a first baseman's mitt, and I didn't even know how to work the fingers on a regular glove. The coaches hit ground balls to me by the hour, and I missed quite a few. . . . I also had trouble throwing. My arm was too strong." But Hank just worked harder to overcome his shortcomings. His effort paid off: After being named Most Valuable Player in the minor leagues, he was called up to the Detroit Tigers' major league team in 1933.

Hank encountered other problems. Although Jews had been playing ball since the start of the game, and other Jewish ballplayers, such as Moe Berg, Harry Danning, Milton Galatzer, and Phil Weintraub, had played in the majors, none had the crowd-pleasing performance or the fame that Hank began to enjoy. Some fans resented his rising star. At the ballpark, people in the bleachers booed him. He was often called insulting names, like "kike" and "sheeny."

The anti-Semitism Hank faced was not confined to the fans. Players on other teams, like the Yankees, and even the owners of the teams also felt—and showed—their prejudices against Jews.

Sometimes he was threatened physically, but because he was so tall and strong, other players didn't want to fight him, and they usually backed down.

For the Jews of Detroit, however, and for Jews elsewhere in America, Hank Greenberg was a hero. Hammerin' Hank or High Henry, as he was called, was making a name for himself. In 1934, led by Greenberg's .339 batting average, the Tigers jumped from fifth place in the American League to become contenders for the American League pennant. It was the first time since 1907 that the team had had a real chance of winning and going on to the World Series.

On September 10, the Tigers were scheduled to play the Boston Red Sox. They led the league by four games. But September 10 was also Rosh Hashanah, the Jewish New Year. Hank was torn. Should he play the game and help his team to win? Or should he take a stand as an observant Jew and spend the day in synagogue? Fans and rabbis hotly debated the question. Finally, Hank came up with a compromise: He played on Rosh Hashanah, hitting the two home runs that won the game, 2–1. But ten days later, he spent Yom Kippur, the Jewish Day of Atonement and the holiest day of the year, in synagogue. The Tigers lost the game that day.

The Tigers did win the pennant that year but lost the World Series to the St. Louis Cardinals in seven games.

In 1935, spurred on by Hank's 36 homers and 170 RBIs (runs batted in), the Detroit Tigers went all the way and won the World Series for the very first time in the team's forty-two-year history. Hank broke his wrist in the second game of the series and had to watch from the sidelines as the Tigers defeated the Chicago Cubs. At the end of the 1935 season, he was voted Most Valuable Player in either the National or American League, the first time a Jewish player had ever had that honor.

For every year from 1934 to 1940—except for 1936—Hank led the Detroit Tigers in home runs. In 1938, Hank was able to challenge Babe Ruth's record of hitting 60 home runs in a single season. With only five games left, Greenberg's total was 58. Would he be able to do it? Baseball fans all over the world watched and waited.

But Hank never got the chance to beat the record; several pitchers in those last, crucial games chose to walk him. While Hank was prevented from breaking the record set by the Babe, he still set a record for the most multi-homer games—11—in a single season. He wasn't bitter about not breaking Babe Ruth's record; instead, he was happy to have gotten as far as he had.

Babe's record stood until 1961 when Roger Maris of the New York Yankees hit 61 home runs. In 1998, Mark McGwire topped that number with a new record of 70 home runs. And in 2001, Barry Bonds broke that record with 73 home runs in a single season.

On December 7, 1941, Japanese troops bombed Pearl Harbor. The country was horrified. The United States entered World War II by declaring war on Japan and its ally, Germany.

Hank became the first major league player to enlist. While he could have had a safe job in the U.S. as an athletic instructor for the army, he chose to serve in the Army Air Corps, and asked to be sent overseas. He first went to India, and later to China. "I'll never forget the first mission our B-29s made from our base to Japan," Hank told

a reporter for the *New York Times*. Hank was in the control tower when the planes took off. "Then we spotted one fellow in trouble. The pilot saw he wasn't going to clear the runway, tried to throttle down, but the plane went over on its nose at the end of the field." Along with another man, Greenberg raced to the burning plane to see if they could help. "As we were running, there was a blast when the gas tanks blew and we were only about 30 yards away when the bomb went off." Miraculously, no one, not even the pilot, was hurt.

When the war ended in 1945, Hank had not played baseball for four years. People thought he wouldn't be able to play the way he had before. But Hank returned to the Tiger lineup and hit a home run in his very first game back. He then went on to lead the Tigers to another World Series victory that year. And he personally clinched the American League pennant with a grand slam home run on the final day of the season.

The following year, Hank married Caral Gimbel, whose father owned the famous Gimbel's Department Store. They had a daughter and two sons, but later divorced. Hank then married Mary Jo DeCicco, who had briefly been an actress. Hank and Mary Jo remained together for the rest of Hank's life.

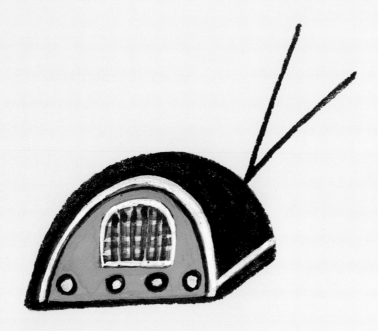

Hank was earning a lot of money as a ballplayer when he got into a salary dispute with the owners of the Tigers. He decided to retire rather than play for less money. But if Hank retired, the owners of the Detroit Tigers would lose money. So instead, they traded him to the Pittsburgh Pirates. Hank was insulted that he had not been told of the trade in person. He heard the news on the radio.

At first he was so angry he wasn't going to play, but the Pirates coaxed him into playing the 1947 season. He had a new contract that made him the highest paid player in the National League. The team's co-owner was the famous singer Bing Crosby; Crosby recorded a song, "Good-bye, Mr. Ball, Good-bye," with Hank himself and the comedian Groucho Marx to celebrate Hank's arrival. The Pirates also moved in the seats in Forbes Field's vast left field, to accommodate Hank's pull-hitting style. It was quickly renamed Greenberg Gardens.

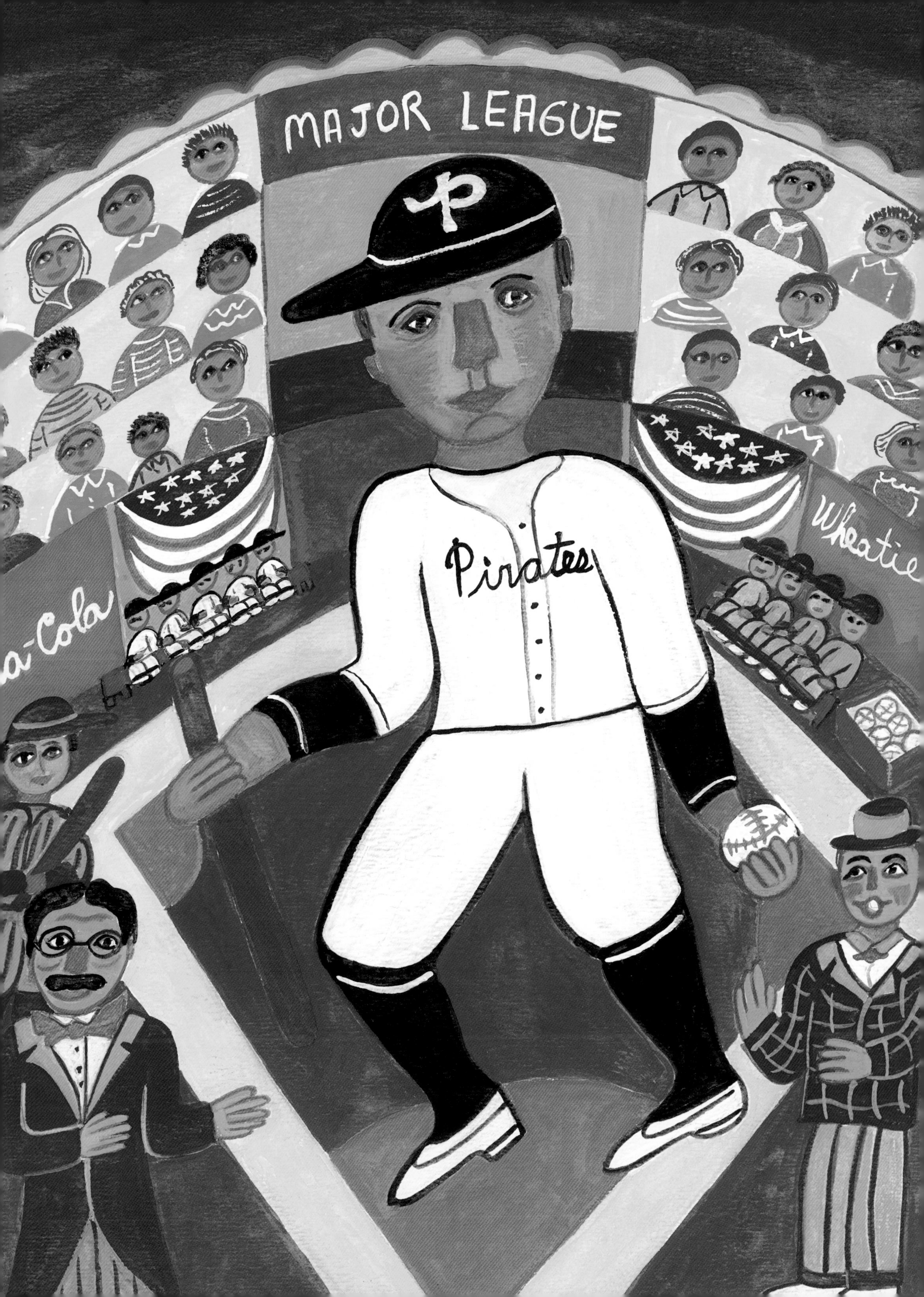
MAJOR LEAGUE
Pirates
a-Cola
Wheatie

During a Brooklyn Dodgers–Pirates game, Hank collided with a young player named Jackie Robinson. Jackie was the first black man in the major leagues. Later, Hank asked Jackie if he had been hurt on the play. When Jackie assured him that he was all right, Hank replied, "Stick in there. You're doing fine. Keep your chin up."

Like Hank, Jackie was often taunted by the insults hurled at him by players, teammates, and fans. So he appreciated Hank's encouragement. "Class tells. It sticks out all over Mr. Greenberg," Robinson commented to a reporter from the *New York Times*.

Hank understood how the younger player must have felt: "Jackie had it tough, tougher than any baseball player who ever lived. I happened to be a Jew, one of the few in baseball, but I was white. . . . I identified with Jackie Robinson. I had feelings for him because they treated me the same way," Hank recalled in his autobiography. He was one of the few opposing players to give Jackie his support.

The next year, Hank retired from the playing field. He became the first Jewish general manager (for the Cleveland Indians) in baseball, helping the Indians win a record 111 games in 1954. In 1956, Hank was the first Jewish player inducted into baseball's Hall of Fame.

In 1959, Hank and Bill Veeck purchased the Chicago White Sox, making Hank the first Jewish co-owner of a major league team. That year, the White Sox won the pennant for the first time in forty years. In 1961, Hank retired from baseball altogether and began a career on Wall Street as an investment banker.

He had paved the way for other Jews to join the top ranks of major league baseball, such as Hall of Fame player Sandy Koufax, player/general manager Al Rosen, and owner, and now commissioner of baseball, Bud Selig of the Milwaukee Brewers.

Hank had been healthy and strong for most of his life. But in 1985, at age seventy-four, he learned that he had a malignant tumor on his kidney. Although he received treatment, his condition grew worse. Hammerin' Hank finally set down the bat for good the following year, when he died quietly in his sleep.

HANK GREENBERG'S VITAL STATISTICS

Height: 6' 3 ½"   Weight: 215

Threw and batted right-handed

Led league in home runs: 1935, 1938, 1940, 1946

Led league in runs batted in: 1935, 1937, 1940, 1946

American League All Star: 1937, 1938, 1939, 1940

American League Most Valuable Player Award: 1934, 1940

Elected to the Baseball Hall of Fame: 1956

CAREER
Games played in: 1,394

Batting Average: .313

Home Runs: 331

Runs Batted In: 1,276

WORLD SERIES
Games played in: 23

Batting Average: .318

Home Runs: 5

Runs Batted In: 22

CHRONOLOGY

January 1, 1911: Born Henry Benjamin Greenberg in New York City

September 14, 1930: Signed with the Detroit Tigers, but would not be called up to the major leagues until 1933

1933–46: Played with the Detroit Tigers

1935: Led the Detroit Tigers to a World Series Championship over the Chicago Cubs

1938: Falls short of Babe Ruth's home run record by two home runs

1941–45: Served in the United States Army

1945: Led the Detroit Tigers to a World Series Championship over the Chicago Cubs

1946: Married Caral Lebworth Gimbel

1947: Played with the Pittsburgh Pirates for one season; retired as a player at the end of the season

1947: Glenn Greenberg is born

1948: Stephen Greenberg is born

1949–1957: General Manager of Cleveland Indians

1952: Alva Greenberg is born

1956: Inducted into United States Baseball Hall of Fame at Cooperstown, New York

1958: Divorced from Caral Gimbel

1959–61: Part owner of the Chicago White Sox

1961: Retired from baseball

1966: Married Mary Jo DeCicco

September 4, 1986: Died in Beverly Hills, California

GLOSSARY

BALL—A pitched ball not swung at by the batter that fails to pass through the strike zone.

BATTING AVERAGE—The number of times the batter is able to hit the ball out of all the times he's at bat. For instance, if a player goes to bat four times in a game and hits all four times, he's batting 1.000. If he goes to bat four times and only hits twice, he's batting .500. A good batting average is anything over .300.

GRAND SLAM HOME RUN—When there are already runners on each of the three bases and the batter's hit is able to bring them all successfully to home plate.

HOME RUN—When the batter hits the ball and is able to go around all three bases and reach home plate without being tagged.

MAJOR LEAGUE—The highest level of U.S. professional baseball.

MINOR LEAGUES—Teams of professional players owned by the major leagues that often serve as training grounds for the majors.

PENNANT—There are two divisions: the American League and the National League. Each one has a first-place winner, and that team wins the pennant. The two pennant-winning teams go on to play in the World Series at the end of the season.

ROSH HASHANAH—The Jewish New Year, a joyful holiday spent in synagogue and marked by a special dinner.

RUN—When the player makes it to home plate.

RUNS BATTED IN (RBI)—When the batter hitting the ball allows a player already on base to score.

STRIKE—A pitched ball that is in the strike zone or is swung at and is not hit fair.

SYNAGOGUE—The name for the Jewish temple or place of worship.

WALK—When the batter is allowed to reach first base after taking four pitches that are balls.

WORLD SERIES—The World Series is a series of seven games played between the American and National League champions.

YOM KIPPUR—The Day of Atonement. Observant Jews fast for a period of twenty-four hours and spend the day in synagogue praying. Yom Kippur is considered the most holy day of the Jewish calendar.

BIBLIOGRAPHY

Crisfield, D. W. *The Louisville Slugger Book of Great Hitters*. New York: John Wiley & Sons, Inc., 1998.

Dickey, Glenn. *The History of American League Baseball Since 1901*. New York: Stein and Day, 1982.

Falls, Joe. *The Detroit Tigers: An Illustrated History*. New York: Walker Publishing Company, 1989.

Greenberg, Hank. *The Story of My Life*. New York: Random House, 1989.

Kisseloff, Jeff. *Who Is Baseball's Greatest Hitter?* New York: Henry Holt, 2000.

Reidenbaugh, Lowell. *Cooperstown: Where the Legends Live Forever*. New York: Crescent Books, 1993.

Sullivan, George. *Twenty-Seven of Baseball's Greatest Sluggers*. New York: Atheneum, 1991.

J. ERSKINE MAY
P. PHILADELPHIA NATIONAL

MORRIS (MOE) BERG

BIG LEAGUE CHEWING GUM

"BUDDY" MYER

LA

AUSMUS

Houston Astros

KEN HOLTZMAN

C

CUBS

AL ROSEN
CLEVELAND INDIANS

RED SOX

R

KEVIN YOUKILIS